Dedication

To the one I love

This one is for you!

The Luminescent Heart

A Poetic Journey of Life's Musings

By

Archbishop Tony Scuderi, NOSF, DD, JCD, DMin, PsyD

Welcome to my journey,

One of life's beautiful gifts is to share one's heart with those who are trusted and will not take vulnerability as a means to devalue or deliberately use it as a weakness. Each of us has feelings and emotions. We have hidden fears and joys. A poetic journey of life's musings is a compilation of my experiences as I interacted with, befriended, loved, and enjoyed a self-illuminating life. I hope this book is a journey that hits deep within your heart. Allow your vulnerabilities to come through as you read these poems. I guarantee you will learn so much about yourself. As I was writing this, I experienced a full range of emotions, from laughing hysterically to having a heavy heart, reliving memories of a time that I wish never went away, and moments of great sadness and loss filled with tears. At the end of this book, I experienced a sense of calm that remarkably gave me peace and hope for a better tomorrow.

As you read these poems, take a few moments to see if any relate to your experience. Then, share with me the emotions that come as we both share a Poetic Journey of Life's Musings. With Love.

Tony

Table of Contents

Part 1: From the Heart 10

From the Heart... 11

In the Silence of my Room.................................. 12

In the Moment.. 13

Our Book of Life: Journeys................................. 15

Why?.. 16

The Journey Along the Way................................ 17

Judo Gold.. 18

As Years Wave Goodbye.................................... 20

Don't Lose Your Mind.. 22

It's Your Day... 23

You're that Gift To Me..25

¡ Escuchar !... 26

A Mind at Rest.. 28

Changing Times.. 29

I Left You A Church.. 31

Rainbows and Roses... 33

The First Pilot's Dream....................................... 34

Part 2: Meaningful Words.. 38

    Health.. 39

    Home.. 40

    Purpose... 42

    Community.. 43

    Grace... 45

    Cats.. 47

    Friends... 49

    Purpose... 51

    Heaven.. 53

    Guitar and Flute.. 54

    Books... 56

    Faith... 58

Part 3: Lyrics of the Heart....................................60

    The Ballad of Uncle Ted................................. 61

    The California Waltz..................................... 64

    Where Have You Gone?.................................... 65

    You Make me Happy, And I am all Aglow...... 67

    Lyrics of the Heart..................................... 69

    The Orchid's Song....................................... 71

    Tomorrow's Melody....................................... 72

Philadelphia Sky..................................... 74

Travelin' with the Bishop........................ 77

The Ballad of Luminescence..................... 81

Part 4: Perfect Joy **86**

In Good Times and in Bad Times............... 87

Lemon Drop.. 89

Perfect Joy... 91

From the Heart...................................... 92

Part 5: My Children, My Pets................. **94**

My Children, My Pets.............................. 95

Snoopy, my boy..................................... 97

Ode to Hepsebeth, Jane Francis, and

Nyota... 99

Grandma Osa.......................................101

To Toby...104

To Noah.. 106

Companionship..................................... 108

Part 6: Fantasies................................. **109**

Part 7: Beginnings............................... **115**

"It all starts here".................................. 116

"First Steps"... 117

"Learn Well" 118

"Days End" 119

"Dreams" 120

"Awakening" 121

"Work" 122

"The Drive Home" 123

"To Dine with Love" 124

"Children at Play" 125

" Slumber" 126

"The Weekend" 127

"Secrets" 128

"Summer" 129

"Winter is Here" 130

"Spring" 131

"Fall" 132

"Beginnings" 133

Part 7: Life's simple pleasures.................................**134**

"You" 135

"Leisure Time" 136

"Returning Here Whenever You Can" 137

"Bar-B-Que Roast" 138

"Success" 139

"Many Days" 140

"Around the Pool" 141

"It Takes a Village to Create Success" 142

" A Walk in the Park" 143

" Let's do it Again" 144

" Puppy Dogs" 145

"Holdin' Ya Sweetly in my Arms" 146

"Life's simple pleasures" 147

Part 8: Challenges **148**

" Stand Tall" 149

" To Give Thee" 150

"Conscience" 151

" Fortitude" 152

"Never Say Goodbye" 153

" Both Have Won" 154

" Now You Decide" 155

" Complete" 156

" Fairwell" 157

" God and I Love You" 158

" Challenges" 159

Part 9: Wisdom.. 160

"The Beginning of Wisdom"............................ 161

"Choice" 162

" The Seat of Wisdom"...................................163

"The Joy of Wisdom"......................................164

" The Making of Wisdom"............................... 165

" The Great Wise Man".................................. 166

" The Great Wise Women"............................... 167

"The Seeker of Wisdom"..................................168

"Sophia" 169

" Divine Wisdom"... 170

" Wisdom"... 171

Part 10: Haiku... 172

"Ran (Orchid)" 173

" Chō (Butterfly)".. 174

"Yanagi no ki (Willow Tree)"............................ 175

"Maiagaru Washi (Soaring Eagle)"............... 176

"Geisha" 177

"Doragon (Dragon)"...................................... 178

" Tora (Tiger)".. 181

" Uma (Horse)"... 182

" Tori ni esa o yara (Feeding bird)"............... 181

" Bushi (Samurai) "................................ 182

"Kirihanasenai (Inseparable)"........................ 183

" Inochi ni Goburetto (Goblet of Life)".........184

" Gorudofinchi" (Goldfinch)................................185

" Taida" (Sloth)...................................... 186

" Botan" (Peony)................................... 187

"Omu" (Parrot)................................... 188

" Sukikyo" (Cardinal)................................. 189

"Heza" (Heather)................................ 190

" Temgoku" (Heaven)................................191

" Taiyo" (Ocean)................................ 192

" Gajumarunoki" (Banyon Tree)...................... 193

" Shimauchi" (Island)............................. 194

" Altar"(Saidan)................................ 195

" Ni Wanotori" (Two Birds)............................ 196

" Tomodachi" (Companion)................... 197

"Oi" (Throne)................................... 198

"Buru" (Bull) 199

"Terasu" (Illuminates)......................... 200

About the Author.. 201

Part 1

From the Heart

From the Heart

Deep, deep inside, where no one must go,
Lies hidden secrets, and dreams where desires flow.
With passion and love life's wind does blow,
Giving our mind wisdom and the power to know .

They say it's the seat of love so divine,
Something to give away all of the time.
It's hard to protect or, to share what is mine,
But it gives us pleasure, and sometimes makes us whine.

Yours is mine, and mine is yours
It is that thing that opens many doors.
Giving us promises and hopes to store.
And a way that leads us too much, much more!

In this place so safe is where honesty starts,
And Cupid's arrow hits like a thousand darts,
A place with no lies, and true love never parts
This place says, "I love you," And it's all from the Heart.

In the Silence of My Room

Surrounded by books on the shelves they sit

Hundreds upon hundreds a few can't fit.

On the top shelf sits photos of the past

Memories of Mom and Dad, Neah my dog who a few years passed.

Stuffed animals, two globes and a wooden plain

The Spirit of St. Louis and a Cessna pen set remain

Fond memories of the past my mind retains.

Upon my desk rests my doggie Noah on his bed,

Next to my computer screen with lots of thoughts in my head.

Toby my other is resting at my feet,

I ponder and stare looking around with tears that meet

Oh, how I wish life were not so quick

wishing the pain and the heartache would stop making me sick.

But, in the sound of the silence, in this quite little room,

I find solace and peace,

Feeling alone and very much at home.

But, deep in my heart,

Where I can only go,

There is peace and there is joy

With sweet music that flow

This is my place where my mind can bloom

And it can only be found in the silence of my room.

In the Moment

In the moment, in the quiet embrace of a warm afternoon,
Lounging with the distant sounds of the world's swoon,
I sit here gazing at the vastness of blue skies above,
surrounding the earth and the moon.

Realizing the illusion, that what I see, is a safe covering,
guarding us all from space's dark sea.
And in silence, I sit, without a sound and no one around with
a Carignan resting next to me.

The silence soon broke; a cargo plane glided by.
See, she never swerves or falls or rises, but straight and
level she rides.
With strength and power, held tightly inside, held up only
by that which seems to hide.
Surrounding the enormous, heavy, powerful, instrument of
flight gliding with grace and tremendous might. Does the
wind control her, or does she capture and control the wind
with her might? ...
Or...

Maybe a little of both, that which is unseen, controls that
which is seen, and that which is seen attempts to
capture and control that which is unseen, an interesting
thought to ponder and dream.
What I do witness in the musing of my mind is that both
work in concert and they mark good time! All I do know is
that both must possess a willingness to give and take,
where the powerful yields to the unseen, and the unseen
lifts up the powerful, traversing through time where
occasionally they meet...

But wait....

A distraction in the world causes a break in the wonderment of the silence. Not a sound, nor a whisp of the wind, nor the voice of a person, just stillness within.

Alas! The music of a Whippoorwill, the sound of Goldfinch, then out of the newly budding trees hops the Jaybird, the Sparrow, and a Red Winged Blackbird. All break the silence singing joyfully this day, welcoming Spring singing the winter away.

Seeking stealth and quiescent steps among the new budding trees they find a limb, a perch to test. They soon build a home to live with a mate, a safe place to nest, to have a family, to grow and to rest.

As Spring times comes and blossoms bloom, the cold of Winter past, the world awakes from its somnambulance, with silence, reminding us to keep the past.... Past!

Now into the future a new journey begins, with the world around us holding her secrets within.

Traverse! I say, go boldly and proud! Step into the future and join the crowd! Take my hand and let me guide you through this tumultuous land. For the sun will rise another day, and the moon will shine at night. The dawn will call the birds to flight, with eyes wide open, I hold so tight the joys and the sorrows of the world's luminescent light, till nightfall comes we welcome a restful delight.

Our Book of Life: Journeys

We all have our stories and journeys to tell.

Some take us to heaven; others take us to hell.

But the stories are all true and the journeys went well,

Recording them in our book of life, that never should we sell.

A record we keep of all we do and holding our secrets close to our heart.

It is here that our dreams and life's journey start.

Our work we have chosen as our crafted art,

Touching us with sweetness and never tart.

With one foot in front and the other close to follow

Amidst muck an and mire worth nothing and so hollow

I toss it away, with tears that never wallow

With no fear and the strength of the god Apollo.

And this day as always another page is turned

Only to live life and know that I'm free.

No one to stop me, no one but me,

Why?

"Why" is such a question!

Never ask me "why?"

Open ended as it seems,

It has no answers to your dreams.

Someone said if you ever want to know,

Then, "why" is the way to go!

But asking "why" surely doesn't know

The who, what, when, where, and how, show

And so, one day I asked a teen

Who drank a bit of Jim Beam

Why he thought it was OK

"Because!" Is all he had to say!

And though "why" is a query some word,

An answer it does not give.

But ask who? What? When? Where? or how?

Then sit back for a complete answer now.

The Journey Along the Way

What is this journey I need to take today?

I want to pack some things and just get away!

The spirit within is restless as can be,

And curiosity is getting the best of me.

Shall I go to the shore, or the mountain road I adore?

Should I take some wine, or just find a place to dine?

Or simply solicit subdued sounds of silence in the deep
wooded pine?

What shall I take as I traverse the world today?

Not just my thoughts, or classical music to play.

I must take on this journey, the depth of my soul to start

And the gentle love and desire that rests softly in my
heart.

Alas, dear thoughts, seeing things the eyes cannot.

Musing secretly in quiet dreams a reality the world knows
not.

Yet, ablaze with excitement and unbounded joy I feel

With eyes poised to the heavens, experiencing all that I can
steal.

The Journey along the Way has been

A gift of love deep within

As my being succumbs to peace and rest

I return to reality renewed, refreshed and blessed.

17

Judo Gold

Along the gentle path, I tour
Remembering the cheers and tears throughout the
years
Tossing and being tossed on the Judo floor.

I relegate those thoughts to me
Not conceded nor egotistical, you see,
But memories of a time spent in agony
Of years of practice and pain and lots of ecstasy.
From Shiro to Shodan and far, far beyond
From student to master, my life in Judo lives on.

From day to day and year to year
My techniques I practice with strength and no fear
Learning them all without a tear.

From Sensei to Sensei, as the years go by,
I have become a teacher and Judo guide.
And this promise I make to all concerned,
The Judo I teach will be free to learn,
And hard to beat, my credibility will be complete.

For if I fail by disrespect and pride
My Judogi, I shall hang up and never more shall fly.

So, I dedicate these dreams and years
These wisps of cheers, The pain and fears
The tears of joy, throughout the years
To all in judo, myself as well
With best wishes, and may we all enjoy...
The harmonious development and eventual perfection
of our human character
That we embody so bold
And this we call
Judo Gold.

As Years Wave Goodbye

Everyone has a timeline,

All are greeted at the beginning and bid farewell in
the end.

And as the years move forward, little mind do we pay

On where the past is going, and where the future lay.

Before we know it, for a moment time stands still.

It's that age where we look back through our
memories and will,

With swift smiles remembering all those thrills.

Picture books and flashes of things we did

Looking at our loved ones in our minds they still live.

We remember their youngness, virility and spunk.

Their jokes and their uncanny luck.

We muse on their wisdom, hearing their voice so dim,

Yet, in the depth of our being lies that sacred wind.

A tear in the eye abruptly comes,

Wishing for the past, yearning to be young.

And yet, here we sit, with years behind,

Remembering times with a good red wine.

And so, a glass I raise to thee so high,

Some surreptitious thoughts that make us wonder why,

Yet bring smiles to our face

As the years wave goodbye.

Don't Lose Your Mind

You saw her in the distance, Your eyes could not move.

Capturing her beauty, In her silhouette you muse.

Lost in a world only the two of you know,

As you wonder if she notices you,

Or, are your feelings hidden, too?

Don't lose your mind, the day is still young.

Dream of wrapping your arms around her in the noon day Sun.

The shadow of her smile, the star light in her eyes.

Yet, Nothing really matters, when she is by your side,

Time is standing still, capturing your heart, brand new.

Her perfume's precocious precautions,

Perfectly pretending to part,

Don't lose your mind, the fun is about to start.

The distance now is close, space begins to join,

Two hands, two hearts, two lips do meet

In sweet silence is heard the quiescent beat

Don't lose your mind

Simply acquiesce to the heat.

It's Your Day

When we were only one, the world we would explore

We started our journey just crawling on the kitchen floor.

Our head looked straight, 'till it lifted to see you approach from the open door.

And soon we stood and walked, we tied our shoes, we went to school

And we experienced much, much more...

When we were twenty-one, that brief yet magical year,

The world we once explored, was now very near

We grew so quickly, we loved so well, we maybe went to college

Exploring the world's wishing well...

And we continued to experience, much, much more...

When we were forty something, the world we really knew

We've experienced life and celebrated the red, white and blue.

23

And as we looked around, the world is different somehow,

Our head is up, looking, and sometimes lurking in the clouds,

And we ask ourselves, how?...

And we continue to experience, much, much, more.

And in the dawn of our life, with years traversing by,

Bidding farewell to the past, but do we really say, "goodbye?"

And as the days grow shorter and life's journey begins to slow

We look at those we grew along the way giving them an awesome show,

Welcoming them to their journey

Telling them, "it's your day," now go!

You're That Gift to Me

Sunlight on the meadow, Picturesque it is to me,

Observing diligently the dancing willow tree.

And look, a bit in the distance three deer do appear

A Buck, a Doe and Fawn so rare.

There's life abounding all around me

Delightful and charming to see

But the best of all is I have you here with me.

The Dew is setting this evening, shimmering as the sun does set.

Wispy clouds and colorful skies

Just like those on the day we met.

The gentle warm breeze surrounds us as the evening draws close,

With a heartfelt arm caressing your waste

And yours around me grasping gently in haste.

And as we gaze into each other's eyes

Watching the stars dance in the sky over a cup of brisk hot tea

My mind constantly reminds me, you're that gift to me.

¡Escuchar!

¡Escuchar! Listen! Listen to you!

Deep in your heart there is something calling, trying to
come through

What is this feeling? It is something brand new.

¡Escuchar! It is calling you.

I feign at its beckoning, so foreign to me

There is no choice but to listen to that deep within my
entity.

Is it a challenge calling out to me

A challenge leading to my true destiny?

¡Escuchar! Quiet! Won't you please?

Your speech makes too much noise.

Be still and listen to me!

As I lead you deeper and deeper into yourself

Look around you and gather the world's greatest
wealth.

Your mind and your heart are joined together you see,

But sometime your stubbornness overtakes me.

¡Escuchar, Me amigo y usted!

Listen to me, you are my friend.

I live deep, deep within you, and we talk now and then

You ask me questions, and get answers, my friend

I tell you I love you, that will never end.

I am your very soul, together we blend.

A Mind at Rest

Tumult and timidity two threads to thrash!

Fighting ferocious fantastical facts,

'midst mindful muttering, mystically mismatched.

Racing, rampant, resurgent regrets

Speed. Stop! Slow. Surpass

A mind not stopping, needing to rest!

Alluring, allocating, ambitious attacks

Momentously moving monumentally maxed.

Look! Lovely, lavished lilies

Frenetic flowery fields flamboyantly free

Calming clouds culminating clamorously

Too much to envision. My mind needs to rest.

Slow, subtle, sometimes silent sequestered seats

Belittled, beguiled, befuddled at best,

Quiets things down and puts a mind at rest.

28

Changing Times

Remember when you were a child? What was the world like back then?

In my day gas was a quarter, and cheaper eggs came from the hen.

We started with short hair; then the youth rebellion came,

The next thing we knew long hair became the name of the game.

Mom and Dad looked so young; thought they'd never get old.

And, oh, that music.... From 50's rock and roll.

Time traversed and busy is all we became.

Never thinking of time, believing things were the same.

Some of us took the place of Mom and Dad,

As we made our own families and watched our children grow; we felt sad.

The clothes look different now from what they did back then,

Laughing at our photos wondering what we were thinking when we were ten.

But today is a new world, a lot has changed again.

And, somehow we keep saying, "it was simpler back then."

Yet as we recall the times long past,

The tumultuous remembrances seem to last and last.

We may not understand what the kids do and say sometimes

We shake our head in confusion studying the paradigms,

As we look at our children, and the world's changing times.

I Left You A Church

Once there was a man who lived in Galilee.

A special carpenter crafting gleefully.

His foster father was named Joseph and his mom was
Mary.

Together they grew and built the world into a family.

Joseph gave him God-sense, Mary gave him love

Both knew his specialness; he was as gentle as a dove.

They gave him the name of Jesus a special kind of son,

Teaching him Talmud and Torah was lots of fun!

Then one day, Joseph passed away.

Sadness and loneliness never kept Mary and Jesus at bay.

For Jesus loved his mother, unto this very day.

But, like all young men, he soon went away.

Mary kept her house and friends, while Jesus gathered his
twelve.

From Carpenter to Preacher teaching all lands about God,
love and hell.

Into town and village, curing sick and raising the dead

Went Jesus and his Apostles, full speed ahead.

31

And then came a time when anger and jealously grew

From people who were scared and narcissistic, too.

They set Him up for failure and hung him on a tree.

And, raising His eyes to the heavens where His Father created all

Prayed for those who killed him, while the crowd around Him stood in Awe.

And when His job was finished , He bowed His head in death.

But little did the people know our life is one big test.

For three days hence, from cross and to the grave,

He rose and told us all; no longer are we sins slave.

Still there is that confusion that stops us in a lurch,

With our mind's mystical illusion, scholars attempt research.

What did Jesus leave us, hopes and dreams that merge?

Or maybe a burning heart with doubts that we must purge.

If we listen carefully and look enthusiastically from our perch

We will hear Jesus telling us,

"My children, I left you a church."

Rainbows and Roses

Rainbows and roses, bright colors and smells

Willow trees in the distance and ringing church bells.

Puff clouds wisp by dancing in the bright blue sky,

Watching the wind carefully carry the bright butterfly.

These are a few of the joys that shall never die!

When the bird chirps,

When the owl hoots,

When I run through the fields,

I feel only that love lying deep, deep within

And then I just feel... so healed!

The poppies are blooming, the grass is so green,

The heavens are shouting with bright blues, what a dream.

Birds of all colors come out with a song,

And the wind carries their tune you can hear it so strong.

These are a few more joys that will never be gone!

And there in the distance a rainbow does shine,

At the end of its bend a field of roses I find.

Rainbows and Roses life's joys in our view

Sending us love, for me and for you.

The First Pilot's Dream

When I was young I had a dream.

I saw a world that I've never seen.

Watching the birds fly so high,

My desire came to touch the sky.

And, so, one day, I took the risk.

I drove to an airport with flight bag in hand,

Sitting with my chart, I etched out a flight plan.

I told my instructor, "I'd like to take flight."

With a deep vibrating laugh, he said, "hold on tight."

He told me to sit as pilot in command,

After a walk around that safety demands.

My instructor told me to take the yoke in my hand.

We revved up the engine, ready to leave the land.

Down the runway I taxied, Two-Seven by name,

Turning prop into the wind, checking the systems to
ensure no blame.

Then turning again down Two-Seven, the same

The tower cleared me for takeoff, into the sky I
came.

And then, like a serge came a feeling I never had
before

I actually felt my stomach hit the floor.

Yet into the sky I began to soar

With earth below me, blue skies ahead, realizing that
God just opened the door

Nothing around me except blue sky and clouds

The roar of the engine, good grief, it was loud.

A tap on the rudder and turn of the yoke

To the left I was rolling, gently... no joke.

Stepping again on the right rudder this time

Slowly turning, pulling back on the yoke, I gently begin
to climb.

Six thousand feet I level the plain, stopping the turn
on the dime.

Respecting the sky, but this time it's mine.

No ground below me, the wind at my back

Floating on only air, looking at puff clouds as they stack.

"Turn the plain two-seven-zero," the instructor belted out,

Follow the flight plan as you move about.

So gently askew the plain I did turn,

Two-seven-zero, I repeated without a single squirm.

The plain turned so gently, it felt like a dream,

Without the stall siren belting out a scream.

Again, straight and level I flew to my goal

Below me I saw the runway aglow

I spoke to the tower and got the "all-go!"

I turn on to the final, cut back on the engine, and downward I flow.

Closer and closer the earth comes to my eyes.

I now see the numbers and Vasi lights advise

Backing off on the throttle I remember my books

Reminding me to see how the Vasi light looks

"Red over Red the light says your dead."

"White over white you'll be flying all night"

"But Red over White, is perfect and right"

Get ready to land, time to end the flight.

And lower and lower the plane in a controlled stall goes

Until the wheels hit and begin their final rolls.

Flaps are at full, gently pushing on the brakes as the
metal bird slows,

Pulling into the terminal, with my eyes all aglow.

The brakes deployed the planes at full stop.

The flight instructor chucks my shoulder with a coaches'
pop.

"Well done, good sir!" He said with a grin.

And called this flight an aviator's win!

Grabbing my logbook, he signed off the hours with a gleam.

He laughed and told me, "we make a great team".

Good Lord, I was so happy, I thought I would scream,

Knowing I flew, my first pilot's dream.

Part 2

Meaningful Words

Health

Eyes that slowly open from a sound slumber's night.

Inhale the air; awakened by the sunlight.

And from the warm sheets we unwrap without a fight,

Emerge do we go into the world that feels right.

Slipping on slippers keeping our tootsies quite warm

As we venture forward to our showers controlled storm.

From the waters of life do we emerge cleanses and refreshed,

To welcome the day after we are formally dressed.

A cup of coffee stimulates our heart,

For breakfast, I'm gonna have a blueberry pop tart.

Then off I go into the world anew

Knowing that life will not be askew.

The challenges we have and attack with stealth,

Taking in all of life's wealth.

For today we journey sharing a commonwealth

Feeling tenacious and in perfect health.

Home

This is where I live, eight to twelve hours a day

I walk and I greet you with a smile and, "hey!"

Then to our desk where we stay all day,

Helping and working with those miles away.

Sometimes we meet life's ludicrous lairs

With linguistic loquacious obnoxious cheers.

We then stop and laugh with looks and stares,

Going back to our desk and sit in our chairs.

There may be no couch, there may be no beer,

There may not even be a desk for you, dear.

But friends close as family sometime

With as much love and joy that make you smile and
shine.

We do things close together, we challenge each other, too

And sometimes, we say, "I love you."

Though in this space, as intimate it may be,

A distance is kept between you and me.

After eight to twelve hours, we exit this dome

We drive and we ponder miles alone,

I think of the gifts and things that you shown

Knowing deep down withing I have another home.

Purpose

It defines and it brands; It demands we take a stand.
It wants us to master the task at hand.
It's the reason for being. It guides and commands.
It reinforces in us our passions and plans.

Throughout our lives musing on that we hold inside,
Observing and learning as life traverses by.
We see that which intrigues us, internalizing as we go,
Constantly building on all that we know.

Insatiable, intelligent, illuminating, lairs
Inviting us to learn, through cheers and tears.
Sometimes we agree, other times we fight,
Then we sat back and analyzed the plight.

Our detailed excursus, disperses or alerts us
But never gives us a disappointing disservice.
One thing it does, over and over again,
It allows us to find our defining purpose.

Community

What is this thing that calls us as one,

It lurks in the quietness of everyone.

Bringing us together under the sun

Allowing us to gather and never to run.

Peers with like minds, challenge one another at all times

Not always agreeing but noticing the paradigms.

Rendering open hearts and minds, oftentimes

Raising each other up like a picketing sign.

There is one issue I have with this group

It never seems to miss the scoop

When someone is in need or in doubt or despair

They all gather around coming from everywhere.

No one I know will miss an opportunity

To show their support and undying unity

And not a single one of them has issues or immunity,

With not any of them showing the other impunity

How do we define this, is this lunacy,

A group that gives one another immense
opportunities?

Certainly, a group with no buffoonery.

This small powerful group we call our community.

Grace

Grace, grace, dressed in lace
On my knees praying slowly, never in a race.
God's gracious gift sets life pace.

Grace gives me strength
To carry on the task
And it never allows me to wear a false mask.

Grace is given
It is never hidden
Freely dispensed, and holiness driven.

Grace teaches patience
When times are rough and distressing,
Full of surprises, like a turkey with dressing.

But, most of all grace is divine
A relationship that is both gentle, and kind.
It has no guile; it waits its time.

45

Yes, grace is gentle, patient and kind,

And it lives in the heart in all humankind,

Its that gift from God that sets us free,

It's that nurturing that is needed for you and for me.

Cats

Precocious, prodigious, preposterous, who knew?

A mind of its own, and a matching personality, too.

Ever vigilant, sometime hidden, sometimes in plain
view.

It's always allusive, bidding you a fond adieu.

It lurks in hidden corners, and stealth in its search

Crawling..... creeping..... carnivorous croon

With vision so keen, searching the room,

And then with quiet, quintessential, quirks

It pounces and trounces the mouse at work.

"Meow!" it says, with its Chesser Cat grin,

Bringing to you that day's dinner win.

They're cute and so frightful,

Full of joy and some sin.

Regardless of how you feel, when you see one abound,

Look to your left, and to your right the cat will be
around.

Let it out of the house
It trapeses throughout the town.

Yet all loyal cats, jumps onto your lap
They will paw you and rub on you,
Then decide to settle down
for a little cat nap.

Friends

In the still of the evening, arrives a good friend.

Never precocious; there to the end.

I held you and talked to you about the world and her
trends.

'Cause I love you and will forever, until the moon
descends.

In the still of the evening, my arms do extend.

I'll remembers that night that never ends,

The stars in the sky at distances no one comprehends.

we hoped and we prayed that life's timeline bends.

With a heart full of love forever transcends.

The still of the evening is coming to an end

But, before the sun rises, hold me again.

Tell me you love me, please don't pretend.

If ever we hurt one another, we shall quickly make
amends.

From the still of the evening, to the rise of the sun,

To each other's arms quickly we run.

Our friendship for years is second to none.

An unbreakable friendship seen by everyone.

As the years and we grow old in time

Climbing up that ladder to the abyss divine

Who ever climbs first, the other will soon be behind

Friends we'll be forever, and life will be redesigned.

Purpose

I want to make my mark. The purpose of my life.

To leave this world a legacy as I scamper into the eternal night.

It's doing good for someone, not resting till it's done.

Making someone happy, when they feel somewhat shunned.

We need to be successful, and leave the world anew,

This life does give me purpose. What about you?

Shall we rewrite a new life story, or shall we sing the blues?

The purpose of our journey is to walk in each other's shoes.

In life we all have a purpose, it may be big or small.

We also give life purpose, through our personal call.

I'll help you out, you'll help me, too

In this are promises are true.

Personal purpose proposes perpetual pause,

Condescending capriciousness contains callous cause

While wondering whimsical wishes

Brings brightness brilliant brawn.

Through all this philosophical pondering

Is life's purpose insecure?

No one has full certainty, as we knock on life's huge
door.

But purpose gives us meaning

As we traverse from shore to shore!

Heaven

They call it heaven, honey!
Go there without despair.
It stores all our secrets,
And a place where we can share.

No one out there can enter here,
Unless permissions there.
A haven for our treasures,
A place to store our wares.

In prayer we sit in solitude,
Sometimes wording pompous platitudes.
But with genuine certitude,
We weave a web of gratitude.

They say it's where the heart is.
I guess this must be true.
For when my heart and life are fullest,
Is when I'm home with you.

Guitar and Flute

Six strings and wind what wonderful music they bring,

Two different instruments, oh how they can sing.

Bringing joy and excitement to everything.

The sound of the strings as they pluck out a tune

That only the flute can harmonize, at that wedding in June.

Amazing how the guitar and flute can make the couple swoon.

Then it's off to the concert hall to play

Maybe Mozart or Shubert

Certainly, not Doris Day!

With fingers gently plucking, and pursed lips' ensuing a breeze

Notes rise to the heavens,

like a gentle wind dancing through the trees.

The soft and silky music,

like lilies on a pond

Float gracefully from dusk to early dawn.

The magic of these instruments ring, in heaven's realm they sing,

With joy and true thanksgiving

Great happiness and heartfelt joy they bring.

Books

They say, "it's all been written, long, long ago."

They will tell you there is nothing new or much more to know.

Their heads they will wag when you show them something new,

As you hand them a book written by you.

Each word, each sentence, and paragraph, too

Descriptive phrases, photos and names of people, we know not who.

An insatiable hunger the reader possesses,

Whose mind is open and never digresses.

We hunger for knowledge from past ages or now,

Studying how things are created we're amazed and wowed!

New thoughts are created from the flames of desire,

And the books that are written put our minds on fire.

Books make us happy. Books make us sad

They take us on a journey, They can make us mad or glad.

Books tells us dreams of swashbuckling tales,

Of great sea captains and menacing whales.

They can take us to the stars, to planets unknown.

And then they can safely take us back home.

Books are that gemstone, that never leave us alone.

They are inside us, around us, and over us like a dome.

Without books............. We would be all alone!

Faith

Sometimes, life's journey goes awry.

Human frailty is tested and tried.

There are times when we make it, and times when we
fail,

But we in our tenacity stand up and sail,

Believing in something greater, to which we bow and
hail

It all starts deep within that point of insolvency,
intolerance and peace

A strength that lies, deep, deep within

We cannot see it but know it's there when we sin.

It fights, it battles, it heals, and we win!

On bended knee, bowed head we pray

In silence so personal, so vulnerable we stay.

Never feeling abandoned, embarrassed nor ever alone

That feeling is with us, forever calling us home.

Mindful and centered we focus therein

Leaving the outside out, and the inside in.

The more we settle the more we hear

A sweet subtle voice beaconing us near.

With solace and peace, we believe all will be well,

Our life will be different feeling heaven and discarding
hell.

God is within us, have faith my friend,

Never leaving us, but, within us to the very end.

Part 3

Lyrics of the Heart

The Ballad of Uncle Fred

Come, sit, and listen to my story about a man named Fred,

A poor little man, workin' hard to make some bread.

And then came the day to the casino he went to play

came one spin of the wheel that made his entire day.

Not one,

not ten,

but twenty million, Eh?

Well, the first thing you know, little Fred's a 20 millionaire.

His wife and family told him, "Fred, get away from there

keep all the bullion you just made today,

And let's find a new house with lots of land to play.

Trees in the yard,

A nice swimming pool

A big cookin' kitchen and shed with lots of tools!"

So, off to Nevada in a rental car, you see

Cause Fred did figure, " a new one now just ain't right for me."

He wanted to see if Nevada was the place he should be,

And found a new house with the yard, the pool, and trees

The big kitchen, too.

Home cooked meals.

And even a backyard grill.

So, Fred and his wife and three little boys

Moved to Nevada and enjoyed all the new toys,

He wisely guarded his riches, and his kids went to school

And learned the things they needed

To make life for them very cool!

Hard study.

The honor roll.

Bosses of their own.

And here you have the Ballad of Uncle Fred

The little workin' man who keeps his family fed

If it weren't for that one day

In the casino where he played

There'd be another story I'd have to tell that day.

Might be happy.

Might not.

Maybe, he couldn't stop.

For all of us today Fred has one thing to say

"Never stop a dreamin', watch how ya play.

I got lucky that one Spring day

My wife and fam had nothin'

But today we live OK.

In the end, dear friends, it's all up to you

To make your own story and enjoy a little brew.

Homemade that is,

Red Wine or White

Water is also just as good, too."

The California Waltz

You meet me, you greet me, in a circle we dance
three stepping, romancing in a swing to advance.
the dance floor is perfect, and the music's so clear
as we're stepping, romancing
midst California time my dear.

Your brown eyes are sparkling,
and that dress is so fine,
Three stepping, romancing
in perfect California time

Round and round, we step, and we go,
with smiles on our faces, we dance on tip toes
Chelo's are humming and the violin slows.
the space between us dissipates and then it goes.

With arms around each other
amidst joys without faults
We slide on the dance floor
to the great California Waltz.

Where Have You Gone?

Where have you gone? That passion of mine.

Running so quickly with the passage of time.

One day you are youth, today you see an old wine.

Where have you gone? Where are those years so fine?

You look at young faces in a picture from the past

And you wonder where they all are in this future cast.

How many do you remember or think they remember
you.

Where have you gone? Where are those years so fine?

And onto the future with tears in your eyes

Remembering lost loves, remembering good-byes.

We pine for past that will never return

Where have you gone? Where are those years so fine?

Time passages we venture through

The moments become days and passion drives you.

We look to the past; those faces now old

Where have you gone? Where are those years so fine?

Into oblivion our life ascends

We take our passions and loves to their very ends

And always do I remember the past going through
time as it bends.

Where have you gone? Where are those years so fine?

You Make Me Happy, And I am all Aglow!

Today, when I am all alone, resting here at home,

Listening to my heart in my quiet zone, Under my roof's protective dome,

You have set the tone for my mind to roam,

I ask what makes you happy, and in my dreams, I am shown,

'cause you make me happy and I am all aglow.

And somedays, a smile do you bring

A song do I sing, and in my arms I hold you and dream

You make me happy, and I am all aglow.

One day, I saw you in the distance wave,

You called me, and I gave you a loving gaze, and when we met a hug we gave.

Never would I feel so good, for you I have the deepest gratitude,

That is not some useless platitude,

'cause you make me happy, and I am all aglow

I wait for those days, when our lips will meet,

On that day, once again my heart will beat,

You make me happy, and I am all aglow.

There is no day without you my love, no joy, no dream,
no breath

But the thought of you with my eyes closed so sweet,

Races a smile across my lips and reaches to my heart
so deep

You are my all this today, and every day

'cause you make me happy and I am all aglow.

And forever and a day, a smile do you bring

A song do I sing, and in my arms I hold you with all my
dreams

You make me happy, and I am all aglow.

Lyrics of the Heart

Play me a tune, yes a melody sweet,

Today I gander and run the streets,

I chase a rainbow, to find my gold,

I try to find the words to capture and hold,

My mind is ablaze with rhymes and tunes so bold.

Lyrics of the heart have got me sold.

The sun's in my face, the wind at my back,

I walk along a lonely path with my full field pack,

To the sky my eyes gaze where the moon sits in
watch,

Ordering the tides into the great rocks notch,

All is in order, life is just fine,

The lyrics of the heart, beat in melodic time.

Life is just a journey that takes us far and wide,

Sometimes we love it, other times we sigh.

We trapes through the countryside, we gather grain
to eat,

Whistling a tune, hoping it's you I meet.

And when that journey ends someday, a happy person
I'll be,

For I know I have written, and that you will see

The lyrics of the heart, singing in perfect harmony.

The Orchid's Song

A single stem that stands alone

Bright colors shouting claiming the world as her own.

It has a blue flower, that captures the eye,

A color that calls you, so beautiful it can make you cry.

The song of the orchid, the ear cannot hear

But the melody of the orchid to the eye is so clear.

Sing to me gorgeous your song so sweet

Drown my heart with your subtle beat

The orchid stands tall on the table where she sets,

People walking by cannot help but view her silhouette.

Ablaze, she does stand there, commanding with no threat

Her colors ablaze dancing like a melodic minuet.

The song of the orchid, the ear cannot hear

But the melody of the orchid to the eye is so clear,

Sing to me gorgeous your song so sweet

Drown my heart with your subtle beat.

Tomorrow's Melody

Tomorrow when the sun rises, I'll sing a new song.

I'll shout to the heavens; I'll awake the new dawn.

Tomorrow, tomorrow, it soon will be here

Awakening new life, bringing cheer, not a tear and soon
you'll be here .

I'll be preparin' a banquet so fine,

My laugh will be as hardy as a glass of red wine.

Tomorrow, tomorrow, a melody I'll sing

And there with all joy, to you my heart will I bring.

I need to be packing for a flight I'll be taking,

My clothes are all rolled, and my final check is all done.

Tomorrow, tomorrow, my plane takes her flight,

And soon I'll arrive, to hold you with all my might.

I look out the window at the ground down below

We're now flying over mountains capped with white
snow.

There's a tear in my eye, because I have to go.

And the guy sitting next to me, keeps watching his show.

Tomorrow, Tomorrow, I'll sing this song to you

I'll shout it to the heavens, how you love me too.

Tomorrow, tomorrow is right here today

In anticipation I can't wait to see you, and here I will stay.

Philadelphia Sky

Damned hot summers, too cold winters,
Spring time's blossom, fall trees splinters.
Life is busy there, downtown so packed,
SEPTA busses stop, just past the railway track.
There's a guy on the street corner, selling pretzels for
a hack
And you'll always find a friend to give you a pat on the
back.

Philadelphia sky, hey why ain't ya lookin'?
Crystal blue sky and the sun's got ya cookin'
Walkin' briskly on busy streets all day,
Walkin' briskly home where I like to live and stay.

There's time for myself in the back yard to sit,
Nighttime is fallin', I got wood for my fire pit.
As I look up at the sky, I see the sun fallin' quick.
The hot air gets cool, as I light my fire stick
A chuck of fire fluid and a strike of a match
The pit starts a blazin, best you step back.

Philadelphia sky, hey why ain't ya lookin?
Crystal blue sky and the sun's got you cookin'
Walkin' briskly on streets all day
Walkin' briskly home where I like to live and stay.

The sun's all down now, the night so quiet it be

There's a soft gentle breeze blowin' through the
neighbor's willow tree.
A lightning bug flies quick past my eye,
And just for a moment illuminates the night sky.
Then as quick as it came goes the firefly away
Opening up the night Philadelphia sky that was hidin'
all day

Philadelphia sky, hey why ain't ya lookin?
Crystal blue sky and the sun's got you cookin'
Walkin' briskly on streets all day
Walkin' briskly home where I like to live and stay.

The crickets are a chripin, and a star shines so bright
The moons in the heavens lighting the sky all night.
It's a beautiful silence, not like the days' time fight.
But be careful, might get a mosquito bite.
But, you know you're home staring up at the starlight
And you'll always find peace watching dark clouds
crossin' the moon so white

Philadelphia sky, hey why ain't ya lookin?
Crystal blue sky and the sun's got you cookin'
Walkin' briskly on streets all day
Walkin' briskly home where I like to live and stay.

There's noting like the city or the sky up above,
Nothin' like moonlight on the water, with days you just
gotta love.

75

Or the coo of a flirtatious, turtle dove
Knowin' that Philly fits you like a glove.
Reaching for the one good ol' Philly shove.

Philadelphia sky, hey why ain't ya lookin?
Crystal blue sky and the sun's got you cookin'
walkin' briskly on streets all day
walkin' briskly home where I like to live and stay.

Aweigh to my slumber, my bed calls my name.
I close my light on the bedside table, and my eyes all
the same.
Knowin' that tomorrow starts the same old game.
Traffic in the morning and parking just ain't tame.
Wearin' a suit and tie, I look like someone of fame
Except everyone who's workin', we all take the blame.

Philadelphia sky, hey why ain't ya lookin?
Crystal blue sky and the sun's got you cookin'
walkin' briskly on streets all day
walkin' briskly home where I like to live and stay.

Travelin' with the Bishop

On a train bound for nowhere,

I met up with a bishop.

He was decked out in the club car, in tassels red and white.

We took turns a-stairin', out the window in the darkness,

The boredom overtook us, and we began to fight!

He said, Son, for my lifetime, I've been teachin' good church doctrine,

Giving lots of orders and keeping priests in line.

I've learn to hear people's stories, reading into their souls

I've Learned what they did, that got them in sins hole.

He said, "brother, I tell you this true,

If you don't start praying, you're gonna cry till your blue,"

So, he handed me a rosery,

the biggest one I saw,

He waved me a blessing and told me about Adam's fall.

Then he bummed from me my Cuban cigar, and staired
at a bright star,

And soon the ride got deadly quiet, in that stuffy club
car.

And soon his face lost all color,

And he looked me in the eye

He said, "If you're gonna go to heaven, you gotta
know how to fly."

" You gotta know how to hold them, know how to pray
them,

Know when you need them, know when to kneel.

You never guess your gone to heaven, cause hell's just
as close,

There'll be time enough for genuflection,

when the prayers are done."

So, he pointed to my rosary,

The beads were wrapped in gold.

The cross was made of silver,

In my hand it felt so cold.

He waved me a blessing and told me to pray for my soul.

He said...

"Son, You gotta pray those beads often,

If you wanna save your soul.

Cause' God's got your number,

And, the Devil's got no hold."

Every Bishop knows

That the secret to salvation

Is knowin' what to pray,

And knowin, when to go.

Most of life is painful,

Some of life is gold,

And all you can wish for,

Is God greetin' you when you show.

He took a last look at the beads and me, and then he had to go.

He turned back to the window,

Plucked the end of his cigar,

Tipped his zucchetto forward

And nodded off gazing at a star.

But, sometime, that same evening,

The Bishop's soul God took

But, I'll never forget those last words,

I wrote them in my book.

" You gotta pray ten Hail Mary's,

An Our Father in between,

Don't forget the Glory be,

That starts the second stream.

Don't stop, 'till you finish

With that cross there in your hand.

Bless yourself then kiss it

And start all over again."

" You gotta know how to hold them,

know how to pray them,

Know when you need them,

know when to kneel.

You never guess your gone to heaven,

cause hell is just as close,

There'll be time enough for genuflection,

when the prayers are done."

The Ballad of Luminescence

It was life that gave me Umbridge,

To travel far and wide,

In the depth of my beating heart,

And recesses of my wise mind.

It all began one day back then,

Midst a moment of passion

And spark of a life giving gem

Then into the world we all entered in.

We began our journey from a tumultuous push,

From the loins of our mothers,

Freed from the darkness and a safe womb's cush.

Into the arms of mom and dad

Not sure what to do with this lass or this lad,

Born from the love the two of them had.

Then home did they traverse midst wailing and poo,

Our parents looked into the eyes of me and you,

Wondering about our future that no one really knew.

But hand-n-hand we walked,

And journeyed through life's stew.

From babbling to words, we mimicked the sounds,

from lips that once we thought were remarkable
growls,

These sounds soon made sense to you and to me,

Defining life's partiality.

Children learn life's tasks as they journey through,

Seeking nurturance and periodic solitude

With a doating parent, guiding them too.

And then, one day, the safety net blew.

And, off to school, an experience brand new.

We met new friends, some we liked and other we did
not

We began to learn independence and making decisions on
the spot.

With each passing day, older mom and dad got,

Ne're noticed by us, as girl and boyfriends became a
must,

Not really considering who we can and cannot trust.

Then off to High School, new friends to meet, with
challenges and lessons we experience as

a great feat, advancing successes and never retreat.

And older and wiser we do become,

With Mom and Dad still pacing us and calling us Hun.

We continue life's journey on the walk and the run.

Then comes that mystical time when after we learn
to drive,

We experience our freedom

We learn to say good-bye.

From fledgling to eagles we soar to the sky

Off to college we go or find a job to get by,

And then we notice

Age and time ticking on never stopping for anyone, just traversing on.

One day we wake up and see mom and dad gray,

We wonder, we ponder, we become sad and pray,

wondering how those years got away

or how in the world, we just couldn't stay.

Midlife is upon us, mom and dad are long gone,

If we have any children, Independence is their song,

As we see in their eyes our lives are foregone.

Just like that, in the wink of an eye,

The kids are having kids, now we, as mom and dad we sigh,

Sitting, gleefully and sorrily watching the years simply fly.

And, now in old age we sit here alone.

The kids have left us to be on their own.

We think of good times holding each other so tight.

Knowing soon some day we too shall say good night.

But, alas dear friend, time in memorial blends,

We have memories, dreams, and wisdom's thoughtful trends,

Giving us smiles now and then.

The days go bye

The lights grow dim,

In guiding luminescence

We take the final plunge and swim.

And to rest I do go, with you by my side, with the luminescent dream now living heavenly in the sky,

For all eternity? Aye!

Though time in this world is passing away,

With life's somber challenges now gone astray

Time for a new journey, what does the future hold?

Just a luminescent pathway, and a new story to be told.

Part 4

Perfect Joy

In Good Times and In Bad Times

In good times and in bad times, perfect joy can be found.

It's all a matter of perspective, just look for it like a hound.

We begin our journey in life with a wale.

Merging forth from the safety, of Mom's holy grail.

We're needy and wanting so we cry till it comes,

Soon we learn to be patient and realize it can be fun.

We meet good people and call them our friends.

We put our trust in them and sometimes we need to make amends.

And then there are those days when pain and suffering abound.

The fear of if I'll recover, believing comfort will never be found.

We try and we try, we fall and get up, we move in a direction to the sky and also the ground.

In good times and in bad times perfect joy is all around,

Demanding us not to run and pause, holding onto the sad frown.

For when we embrace the pain and suffering

That new perspective of live we experience, and we
start by buffering.

And when we laugh and raise a glass of cheer,

We realize that life will pass, and we will again see
clear.

Run to the pain, and embrace the joy

Play with it as if it were just a toy.

You'll have pleasure for a while, then toss it all away

Only to wake up and play again the next day!

Joy and sorrow are allusions we live,

Perfect joy of the heart is everything we give.

Lemon Drop

Somedays are just too rough, Y'all need to stop the hectic rush.

Pull up a chair and set down beside me,

I got sum'in that'll make you blush.

It warms the innerds

Calms the nerves, it's true.

Brothers and sisters, I got a lemon drop for you.

Five simple ingredients no still is needed here.

Just a little time

And a gallon jug to spare!

We start with top Tequila, Seven Fifty gets it done,

Pour it gently in the jug, walk it; please, don't run.

You don't want to bruise it and lose Tequila's fun.

Next comes the sugar, two cups should be just fine

More if you like it sweeter, less if you wanna save a dime.

Pour it gingerly into the jug, watch it start to shine.

Three cups of water, keep it pure and bring it here

An ounce of orange extract,

to chase out any fear.

And now comes the final recipe you see

Twenty five ounces of lemon juice as pure as can be

Mix it all together, and shake it all about,

And there you have a lemon drop,

Enjoy, but don't forget to stop!

Perfect Joy

Look what stands 'a fore me, A smile does it bring,

My hearts a leapin' lively, like a rushin' brook or stream.

And as it comes closer, I laugh and hoot aloud,

Nothing makes me happier, nothin' makes me more proud.

I take your hand and dance around, looking deep into your
eyes,

And there I find my wanting soul, seeking what is wise.

With silly stories sweetly spoken

The tenor of the moment shall never be broken.

As long as we're together, and the days and nights move
on,

Perfect joy will walk with us, this moments never gone.

We'll sing a song so joyful, we'll kiss so tenderly,

Our hearts will house each other, for all eternity.

Alas! Alas! Perfect joy it be,

Together we find utmost serenity.

And as the days turn into weeks, and weeks blend into
years

Perfect joy we always will have, to vanquish any tears.

From the Heart

Once upon a time ago, in a land so far away,

There lived a little working lad, that gave, and gave,
and gave.

He hadn't much of anything, wanted nothing much to
gain.

He'd run into the village, treating everyone the same.

A wave to the poor one, a wave to the rich,

A smile for the little one, he'd help a tailor stitch.

What little he had; he gave away, complaining not at
all,

He gave them all the gifts from the heart that all
good people saw.

And then one day a query came amidst the evening
star,

Why do you do these things? You give but never
charge.

He stopped for a moment, a second maybe two,

And then from deep down within, a barreling laugh
came through!

"Oh my, dear friend," he said, with a happy tear in
his eye,

" Look around you, man, do you really need to know
why?"

"The world is filled with sadness; I see too many
people cry.

From my heart I pour out gladness, to wipe the tear
from one's eye."

"It's joy I bring, not sorrow. For a moment ever so
short,

Let's turn a frown upside down, let all of them all
report,

No more pain and suffering, giving all a new start,

To share the love and peace we have, is given freely
from the heart.

Part 5

My Children,

My Pets

My Children, My Pets

I've never had children; they tend to scare me.

A twenty year sentence or more did I see.

But even with a wife lonely I'd be

Seeking four legged creatures, to bring happiness,
that was the key.

And so, from childhood till future times pass

My children, my pets we walked through life's
hourglass.

Forever faithful, and loving they be

Never argue, fighting or fussing with me.

The older I grew the more I learned to love

My children and my pets fit in my heart like a glove.

The difference I found between people and pets,

Is that people living longer, but pets no one forgets.

Then comes the day when they all pass away,

Sweet memories burned in the mind, they stay,

Forever, and ever, till time goes away

Hopefully we'll play again happily one day.

I have fond memories of my children, my pets

With only poems and stories and absolutely no regrets.

My heart is heavy, I cry always deep within

Pining for my children, my pets teaching me love once again.

Snoopy my Boy

A long time ago, at home with Dad, Mom and my two Bros,

I wasn't the brightest of the three, the Good Lord knows,

But the youngest of us three,

And happy as can be.

When Dad brought home Snoopy my boy, home to me

With waggy long tail and a smile on his face,

He kept me company and kept up with my pace.

We grew up together until I left for school

Then Dad and Mom kept him home promising to keep him cool.

And then one day, on the college campus I be,

I felt very unsettled deep inside me.

I called Mom and Dad and told them how I felt,

And Dad broke the news that Snoopy my boy's cards were
unfortunately dealt.

Well, the tears came because I was away

I couldn't hold Snoopy as he went far, far away.

I miss my dear friend until this very day,

Hoping and wishing I'd see him along the way.

But never did he show, nor will he again

But memories I have of my dear, dear friend

wherever you are Snoopy my boy

Deep in my heart I still hold your toy

Waiting for that day when we play once again

Snoopy my boy, I'll love you to the end.

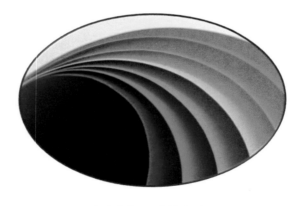

Ode to Hepsebeth, Jane Francis and Nyota

And there she was, a puppy so cute

Sitting in the window all alone, oh my, what a hoot!

Her spots were just coming white and black they would be,

We called Hepsebeth, she was the girl for me.

We took her home from that cage and no fun,

To a loving house where she could run, and run, and run.

Up on the couch, in the yard she'd play

With ice cream and birthday cake on her special day.

The neighbors just loved her and I couldn't get enough,

Of my lovely Hepsebeth, my sweet Dalmatian pup.

She was the craziest you'd ever did see,

My crazy baby was so close to me.

When I was at work, I couldn't wait to get home.

To play with and feed my Heppers a bone.

She soon got a companion with another girl you see,

We called her Jane Francis, and for years they became "we."

Then soon came Nyota, so cute and happy.

Hepsebth, Jane and Nyota and at home with Mommy and Pappy

As I think back on the years so, long, long ago

And oh how I cried when we had to let them go

But Hepsebth, Jane and Nyota love in my heart I will always show.

Till me meet again and enjoy each other's glow.

Grandma Osa

We went to the dog pound to get a new friend,

The wife looked around from pen, to pen, to pen,

... and then went around the bend.

And there she sat with a little gray on her face

A big old girl, alone in one place.

My wife called me up when I came home from work

She said she was on her way home with a message
that possessed a little quirk.

So, we hopped in my car, strange as it may seem

And drove to the dog pound with impetus and mean.

The dear wife told me to, "wait her, I have someone
I want you to see."

So, I waited and waited in anticipation and with glee.

And out did she come with her handler holding a leash.

A lady pit bull mix, a few missing teeth, and the face
of a peach.

Our eyes then met, and her tail did wag

She had my heart when she came to say hi.

Kneeling down on both knees, I swung my arms around
her

And she licked me in my face with glee.

My wife she said, "should we take her, or leave?"

Goading me on, I knew she did tease.

"Good God, of course we'll take her, may I have her?"

I asked her handler, "please?"

Her name is Osa, it's Spanish for Bull.

A name so fitting, quite hefty and full.

She was ten when we got her

An old lady, you see. But the sweetest of sweetest,

Yes, no one is sweeter than she.

She was a true lady until the very end

We think a stroke took her, losing another friend again.

The Vet said there was nothing she can do.

We had to say goodby to dear Osa.

I cried for her, too.

As the years have gone bye musing on all my past pets

Better than humans, never presenting threats.

Growing old is no joke, for human or pet

Here's to you dearest Osa, I am glad that we met.

To Toby

Remember the first time we brought you home.

There in a kennel you were sitting all alone.

Quiet you were, unsuspecting to be,

Yet very observant and calling to me.

It was your eyes my boy, your eye you see,

They looked so lonely, and they followed me.

From the first time I saw, there was joy in my heart,

I knew we had to have you; I knew it from the start.

And so dear Toby a companion you became,

You filled this house with your presence

And we never were the same.

You love to snuggle, cuddle close to me,

You rest in my arms, dear Toby, you never flee.

You're fun to be with, you love your walks in the park
You can't wait for a cookie, and that's just the start.
You're the best in the world, the closest friend to me.
Just ask dear, Toby and I'll give anything to thee.

To Noah

Hey, little boy, my puppy so shy.

Noah, my boy don't panic, don't cry.

Nothing will hurt you, I'll protect you, you'll see.

Come, let me hold you, very close to me.

Leap into my arms, let me kiss you so sweet.

It's OK to hug me, I'll always give you a treat.

A screech from the highway,

A firecracker pops!

At the door in the hallway, you hear a person knock.

You run in a circle, you cry out in fear,

You jump on the couch; you know my lap is near.

Tremble if you must, and cry if you will,

Shhhhh, dear Noah, I'll hold you, be still!

And now all the fear is gone from your castle.

No more will noise be a hassle

It's time for bed, your safe place you find

Slumber dear Noah, Tomorrow will be just fine!

Companionship

Companionship is a word, well defined,

It holds in its meaning promises divine.

It allows for a secret so sublime,

And let's dear friends share a glass of red wine.

Come sit at my table let's talk and dine.

A companion is there in times of need,

They will come to the rescue, at great speed,

With love to hold onto with trust not greed,

Giving life's true message for one to heed.

Ah! Yes! A companion, one to share fun.

Each of us listens, none of us will run.

There to the end, in life till it is done,

Looking deep in her eyes calling him, hun.

That's a companion, in life, worth a ton.

Part 6

Fantasies

Fantasy

It was a cold December's evening,

The sun began to pale.

The darkness covered the land, and silence made the
earth so still.

In the distance there abounded a shape,

Moving rapidly, then stopping, and galloping with a
steady gait.

In front of me came, out of the woods softened earth,

A mist of white fog, creeping, slithering, abounding
with a wide girth.

Into the abyss my eyes did go,

Soon the evenings wispy wind blew cold.

Around my shoulders a blanket I did throw, wondering
where my mind would go.

I looked at the heavens, and the stars all aglow,

To the constellation Orion, Cassiopeia, and yes even a
planet or two to show.

And off to the stars in the ship in my mind,

Oblivious to everything, including bedtime.

Traveling the universe divine, moving through wormholes, diminishing time.

Breaking through to galaxies unknown

Amazed at their colors and a bright golden glow.

Stopping just for a moment, to watch in my mind's eye with thee,

The planets in motion, upon the stars we called heaven's sea.

Through tumult, and tide, tandem torrents that hide

Like the current of an ocean, taking all for a ride,

Or maybe like a sled on the snow, as we slide, and slide, and slide.

The swirls of the galaxies to the right and to the left.

They look so distant, so settled and set.

There is not up, no down there in space, just three dimensions in this place,

Allowing us to float with grace.

To the left I look and see something brand new,

There are bright red colors leading to a trail of purple and blue.

In the middle of it all lies a spot so bright

A star glistening with fire and might.

Yet in its flares tearing out like a shot,

An acquiescent flame with no directions blasts forth so hot,

At its center lies her core, ferocious, veracious, tenacious and more.

Flying past my ship's window, into the abyss it roars.

Once again in the tumult there is, still,

No sound, just planets moving at will.

Never have I seen what no one has seen before,

As I fly through my mind's cosmos, good Lord, I want more.

Into the darkness through the fabric of time,

In wonderment around this fantasy of mine.

Traveling into the deep recesses of my mind,

with no calculations, Nor time to unwind

Through colors and blackness craving peace sublime.

I travel in my spaceship; I travel through time.

Finding amazement and eye candy to dine.

The beauty up here, all around where you look,

It is like the finest dish, made by a world renown cook.

Like flavors that blend in the roux in the pot,

Are the sites that I see in my mind that won't stop.

This is my fantasy, crazy as it may seem,

Going to places that no one can dream.

I see only beauty, in colors array,

Witnessing only glory in my heart it will stay

Come with me. Come! Dream with me please,

Welcome to my world I'll make it a soft summer breeze.

I'll hold you so tightly, as we gaze at the stars above,

Together we'll journey, in our fantasy, to find our world of
love.

Part 7

Beginnings

It all starts here.

A speck of energy,

This force unknown,

Compact as it started,

Holding all that we own.

And tighter, and tighter compressing so long;

Squeezing itself.

Holding itself.

Tightening itself.

Containing itself.

As energy compacts, there comes a point,

When in its excitement, no more to contain,

Closes in on itself, yet still...

Squeezing, Holding, Tightening and Containing .

Until one day the tension unfolds, and from its very essence, its containment erodes.

And there in the darkness, light doth showed.

The road to eternity, our life, and our soul.

And in this masterful burst of force, there...

Our journey of life, it all starts here!

First Steps

"Will you go out with me?"

He asks her one December day.

She says, "yes" to his question,

grasping his hand along the way.

Soon, time has gone by past May, June and July,

Then holding her so tightly as he looks in her eyes,

Soon lips sweetly join, and a fond embrace ensues.

Two hearts beating -- no words as they muse.

With gentle tears trickling down like a soft, subtle, spring
rain would start.

The tension grows fiercely, so, they can't be apart,

with love so intense, like a fine piece of art.

Next to each other untethered of clothes,

With arms around the other, passion arose,

gently touching, hugging, kissing, as the gentle breeze
blows.

Nine months have waned by, now.

And a third will come soon.

Then one day with exuberant pep,

The little one takes the very

First steps.

Learn Well

"Twinkle, twinkle, little star,"

we all know this poem thus far.

And yet it beckons us to hold a very high bar.

Challenging us all in school, work and play,

Making us grow, day after day.

And, yes, we make mistakes along the way.

We fall. We rise. We adjust. But never stay.

"The butcher, the baker, the candlestick maker," we
know this poem thus far.

A challenging theme these pros do present,

For all to decide how we will pay the rent.

As the days, and weeks, and years go by

That little star guides us, and the tradesman tries.

So, we grow old. Time fades away.

Only one thing to do.

Learn well along the way.

Day's End

Today is quickly over

And dusk falls slower,

We'll eat some spaghetti,

And drink some red wine,

We'll give a toast to each other

as we both shall dine,

looking up at the evening star, watching her shine.

The sun sets so softly

Amidst clouds wisping by

Farewell as the day's lost

The night is not shy.

The sky in the evening

This canvas awaits,

The cloud colored distance

From the palate creates

Bright red, yellows and purple

Fading off into black

To each other we attend

Kissing good night my darling, at the day's end.

Dreams

Soft, supple sheets.

Silk. Surrounded by surreptitious furtive glances.

Feelings of knowing the unknown, uncertain, uncanny
whimsical dances.

People I've known. Poignant. Pernicious, Presenting pious

Precocious glances.

All so confusing this experience I'm in.

Scenes change so rapidly,

And battles I win.

In a moment uncertain the scenes once again change,

Look! There's a cowboy singing "home on the range."

What's going on here? Am I going mad?

I'm happy, and frightened and just a bit glad.

And with all this confusion, I'm standing on a beam,

Then all of a sudden falling,

Hearing someone in the abyss calling...

Realizing, it was one of those dreams.

Awakening

Under the linens and silk evening sheets
The darkness and slumber retreats.
The blinds on the windows glisten as the sun greets.

Sand filled eyes from slumbers dreams
And a new day arrives with bright yellow beams.
From tempered breaths to the great arousing rise
I greet the morning with coffee and pies.

Rise up O ye bones, rise up and dance,
The dawn is calling you to a festive romance,
Time to meet new people and give this day a chance.
Give those you meet more than a glance.
A smile. A wave. A handshake and prance.

Be honest no faking, a new dawn is awaking.

Work

Arisen from my slumber,

time to break the fast.

A new day has dawned, yesterday has passed.

A cup of coffee, and the morning news

Hearing little more than the world's same old blues.

I don the suit for the job ahead,

Immediately after I fixed my bed.

And off I go after one last bite.

With cars to the left of me, and trucks to the right.

Slowing quickly, starting to gripe.

And now it begins, the lane changing fight.

The interstate's busy, back-ups to the ramp.

The clock keeps ticking, my hands getting damp,

Did I leave on time? Maybe earlier it should have been.

And now I arrive, park the car and walk in.

Only to sit at my desk to see only one perk

And that dear friend is what I call work!

The Drive Home

The day ends at last, and the drama has past,

I hop in the car; turn the radio to blast.

Back out from my spot, on the road there I go

Wouldn't you know, dudes driving slow.

Back on the highway, a half an hour to score

Before my final destination, I must stop at the store.

I buy the items I need and rush out the door.

Again, in my car, on the road I go,

Really? Oh, no! Another dude, going slow.

Going 40, 55, 65 at best

Refuse to go faster, no need for a Cop test.

And there, up ahead, my ramp... Ah, soon to rest.

Pulling into the driveway,

greeted by my dog with his bone.

Alack and alas, that was the drive home.

To Dine with Love

A touch of Oregano, with Parsley we dice,

Some salt and peppers make dinner so nice.

A little spice here, a bit of seasoning there,

Some butter and olive oil accent the pair.

And now to add clams with linguini and white wine

Stir it vigorously, so the aroma can shine.

After a long journey home, tired and alone,

Midst trials and tribulations, these fettered bones shone.

As I sit and I view the frolic of those at play

I dare not move, with love and laughter,

I just want to stay.

And now we all gather, round the table—hey! Don't shove!

Bow our heads to our Creator, the Son Sanctifier and the
forgiving redeeming Dove.

The days journey's ended, troubles far, far away,

With hands wrapping hands like a warm winter's glove

We, as a family sit, and dine with love.

Children at Play

The flames dance so gayly, as we all gather 'round.

Holding you most tightly, with dogs frolicking

As if they were in town.

In a room, there a yonder, just a stone's throw away

We hear a ruckus, some laughter, all want to stay.

A toast to you little ones

Our daughters and sons,

Come here and have a bite of a hot Cinnamon bun.

Then off do you go, when finished and done,

To wrestling, play fighting and no one has won.

And we, two, hold tightly, having our way,

Our hearts beating together

Telling us to stay.

As we sit by the fireplace

Watching the children play.

Slumber

Shhhhhh! My beloved,

No words must be said,

Upon my broad shoulder

Rest thy weary head.

A mind so busy, day after day,

Little rest for the weary

And too much to say.

Close your eyes, my beloved

let the night take its toll.

Feel safe, my beloved

As my arms 'round you fold.

Be not thee encumbered

By those who outnumber

Just take a deep breath, close your eyes

And slumber.

The Weekend

Five days have gone bye, Tumultuous at times.

Racing thoughts, solving problems,

Resolving conflicts, fighting for that dime.

That's now all behind us, 'twill not come again.

Let's drive to the mountains,

Or to the shore that never ends.

Burgers on the char grill with corn on the cob.

All gathered round the table, like one hungry mob.

We sing around the campfire, and dance out of step,

We laugh at each other, with Uncle Bob in his clown
vest.

Last dive in the deep end,

The lifeguard's whistle blows,

And soon we do realize how quickly time goes.

First Friday, then Saturday now Sunday's sun rose.

Only to wait till next Friday

when the weekend shows.

Secrets

We all have them, everyone knows
Some make us happy; others give us woes.
They lie deep in our hearts
And recesses of our minds,
Shaping the world, we live in
Giving perceptions all the time.

Along life's little journey
Footprints we leave behind
Wondering where to turn next
Or how to make a rhyme.
Silent solace slowly soothes,
while times tenacious timeline moves.

I know something that you don't
I can tell you, but I won't
Truth to be told
We all hold secrets.

Summer

School's out! The kids are home.

Mom and Dad's workin'

And little one's roam.

Oh! Don't you worry safe they are

Jumping and frolicking in our big back yard.

The older watch the younger,

The younger plays with the dog,

Both rolling in the grass that grew so tall.

Don't forget to hydrate, the sun's high in the sky

The temperature's roasting at hot 95.

All right kids and doggies in the pool you go

Do the doggie paddle and see if you can beat Romeo.

Amidst laughter, lunch, lunacy, too

Mom and dad come home from work, for fun with you.

Then off to slumber

I know it's a bummer. But just remember

Tomorrow continues Summer.

Winter is here!

The days are getting shorter,

while the nights are getting longer

The air is getting colder

And the grill's a year older.

Grab the mittens and puffy blue coat

Looking out the window, the snowflakes just float.

The temp drops quickly, good lord it's so cold

If it weren't for the fireplace together we'd hold.

A splinter pops out of the bright burning log.

we watched the dance of the fire and a white smoky fog.

Summer's all gone, and Spring is not near.

The wind is so cold it brings her a tear.

I need not convince her that winter is here.

Spring

The ice is melting ,
Giving earth new life.
Birds start singing,
Farewell winter's strife.

The flowers start growing,
Greenness all around.
The days are getting longer,
And the night abounds.

Short jackets take the place of puffy air coats.
And we watch the frozen ice crack
on the river as it floats.

Love is in the air and that's a good thing.
The children are sad listening to the school bell ring
But we all have smiles because
We know it is Spring.

Fall

Can you feel it?

The crispness in the air.

The leaves fall from the trees

A red one, a yellow one I pick up on bended knees.

The breeze is chilling a bit,

The heat of the day was soon gone.

Wispy clouds from ice crystals are formed

where white puffy cumulous clouds danced and
swarmed

The Sun though bright, is just not as warm,

In the distance is seen a brief rainstorm.

The evening's chill reminds us well

Colored puffy jackets the stores will sell.

Soon to be upon us with no leaves on trees

No flowers are blooming, and grass is not green

This season prepares us for winter to come,

As we stand tall

We enter the season we know as fall.

Beginnings

It all starts here and ends with fall

With life's little journey

Experienced by all.

We're born, we grow, we work, we play

The seasons they come

And soon goes away.

Memories we make along the way

Some good, some bad, some.... Well.... another day.

We fall in love, we follow our heart,

We get a vocation and look for God to start.

A game has innings, gambling has winnings

In life we start only with beginnings.

Part 8

Life's Simple

Pleasures

You

From the first day we met,

You had me at, "hi!"

As the weeks went by

My heart never asked why?

My thoughts are ablaze, with images of you,

And a picture I have that still is brand new.

As the days linger on, into weeks, months and years,

Each vision of you brings me to tears.

No, not sadness comes from my weeping,

But longing and love in joy so sweeping,

I experience love, deep enough that my heart is leaping.

Amidst tumult, hard times, confusion and fear,

My life's simple pleasure is having you near.

Leisure Time

Some of us love music
Others read books,
There are folks that enjoy talking
In little coffee nooks.

And then there's the exception
The one who loves sports,
Like basketball, football, and baseball by reports.

It's time for a break.
Get away from it all.
Arise from your seat, you need to stand tall.

The moment is yours where time has no mind
And there you stand with not even a dime.
Yet, happy and carefree you simply unwind
This my friend, we call leisure time.

Returning Here Whenever You Can

Close your eyes, take a long deep breath.

Slowly exhale, put your body to rest.

Another one, please, repeat as you will

Until all that troubles you abates, and you become still.

In your mind's eye, see a field before you

Ablaze with green grass and singing birds too.

Walk gently ahead to the forest that grew

Puff clouds in the sky between spots of blue.

And down the path in front as you walk

To a log on the shoreline next to the river by the tall
cornstalk.

Sit for a moment, and dream if you will

Of peace in your heart, and for a moment life is still.

Now rise from your seat and follow that path once again

Out of the woods into the field ascend.

As you return to the beginning, from whence this journey
began,

Enter life's new journey, returning here whenever you can.

Bar-B-Que Roast

Life is too short, enjoy all that you can.

Starting with breakfast, lunch and dinner

cooked up in a pan.

But when life goes flat, and seems lonely at times,

Search for smoothness, things and rhymes.

When the need to be listened to, and heard by a friend,

When feelings need to mend,

When people seem not to care,

When no one seems or wants to be near

There is always one buddy, sure and true,

Never judging, arguing or blue.

Always watching, with observant eyes on you.

And when the time comes, and you need them the most,

With unconditional love that ain't milk toast.

Comes the dog, man's best friend

To share with you

your bar-b-que roast,

Success

I remember when you caught my attention

when they said I couldn't do it.

Wasting my time falling into a pit.

Sadness came and belief did not fit.

So, I sat and pondered and cried a little bit.

"Up!" "I said, Up!"

I rose up from my sadness and saw it as a way

To take what I do, and practice what I say.

Confusion sets in occasionally with fear,

But then again you were always there.

Taking hold of the challenge and diminished the fear.

No one in this world has to really care.

Tell me I can't and watch as I impress!

No more wasting time trying to suppress.

The more you say I can't the more I say God Bless.

And as I gather these thoughts and drives of mine,

I see clearly now the gifts I possess.

The harder I work the stronger I grow,

No more to guess, never to accept less.

for now, I am a Success!

Many Days

Tick toc, tic toc, goes the coocoo clock.

Don't stop, don't stop, never letting the ball drop.

The hour tolls and the dancers come forth

from their hidden castles behind the wood door.

Tick tock, tick tock as the moments go bye

a minute, an hour, soon the days just fly.

Marking the moments to treasure each other,

with the endearing love of an older grandmother.

Tick tock, tick tock with a melodic cadence

that never will stop.

And here they come, the dancers again,

On the half hour time

a new dance with the chyme.

Tick toc, tic toc how grand life can be

with dancing and chiming and some very fine dining.

Tic toc, tic toc my heart's all ablaze

with love and thanksgiving for many days.

Around the Pool

The weather's hot and there's no more school,

Dad in the backyard playing with his tools.

Mom in the kitchen where it's cool, she ain't no fool!

The Bar-b-que's hot, and there's lots of fuel,

Ah! the steaks on the Bar-B, just wanna make you drool.

The dogs are barking, and the water is cool.

There's laughter, and running, goofy as a fool

Not a care in the world, not here or Istanbul.

It's summertime..........

and the family's around the pool.

It takes a village to create success

It takes true unity to create one success.

It takes one issue to make a mess.

But, life still travels forward nonetheless,

Reminding everyone never to digress.

When I was walking in the village one day

I saw the children playing away

If work and plans weren't here to stay

heck I'd enjoy myself and make one embarrassing display.

But I did have time to watch and learn

from creative little children, round and round they turn.

Holding hands as they swing in circle they sing,

then one of them falls, it's a funny thing,

they picked him up and stopped the swing.

Then as I continue my journey to work

thinking of the children at play.

I stop and turn but only part way

remembering when the circle broke, everyone stayed,

they picked him up and started again to play

But what the children taught me I must confess,

was it takes a village to create success.

A Walk in the Park

The stress of the day keeps us away
always remember this feeling won't stay.

Frustrated and tired I just want to rest,
because sometimes, others can just be a pest.

So, and idea I have to rest this day
I'll hop in the car, and I'll get away.

The sun is still shining
maybe I can go dining.

Ah! better yet
there's something already the world has set.

So, off I go, as free as a lark
For today I take a quiet walk in the park.

Let's Do It Again!

So, you listen to music, and you hear the rhymes,

And you'll dance to the tunes till the end of all times.

You smile and hop and spin all around,

then up you jump and land on the ground.

And with every note and flourish you hear,

with ragtime in the background so easy to bear.

No time for small talk just a step here and there,

drawing closer to your partner without any fear.

Up go your arms, then they flap by your side,

soon grasping your partner for a theatric glide.

One step, then two and three it will be,

a polka or waltz or quick step with spree.

Then comes the time when the music slows down,

with subtle decrescendos we spin round and round.

And then it does end with that one note suspend,

we stop,

out of breath,

pausing briefly,

let's do it again.

 Puppy Dogs

A friend indeed, is all I need
with wagging tail and black leather lead.
Eyes that look up, never away from me
My sweet little doggie, Oh, how I love thee.

When it's time for dinner a wag of the tail
signals his chef it's time for a good meal.
"What is it tonight?" Says he with his eyes.
"Is it lamb, is it beef, for a treat... raw hide?"

And soon after supper, round and round he goes
circling my legs like a cat who knows.
Time to go play, mom and dad
A walk? Oh, the dog park, to meet the new Lab.

And home from our venture on the couch we do sit,
His head on my lap, wagging a tail that just won't
quit.
Soon, off to bed do we go, snuggle close as a mitten
My little puppy dog, in love, we are smitten.

Holdin' Ya Sweetly in my Arms

The green, green grasses of Ol' California

midst the blue skies above

just dancin' and pickin'

midst the flowers circlin' the love.

Can't get enough of the songs in my head

or the joy that lives in my heart

It's bluegrass Sunday and glad it ain't Monday

with the recipe flowing all day.

Got you on my mind, smilin' all the time,

and I'm two steppin'- heel stompin' –

and reelin' round the bend.

ye-ha'in. hand clappin' do-si-doin' for the send

Got this song in my head

and joy in my heart

It's bluegrass Sunda and glad it ain't Monday

holdin' ya sweetly in my arms.

146

Life's Simple Pleasures

How much we take for grant-it

Even more we never see,

The stars dance above us,

The flower and the tree.

A brisk walk in the winter

Maybe snow on the ground,

They're really water droplets, frozen all around.

The crisp mountain stream with water so clear,

The rocky roads of the mountains

to the smooth sands of the sea.

How glorious and romantic

Very freeing it can be,

Never giving us displeasure,

unbounding and free

Life simple pleasures

A divine gift for you and for me.

147

Part 9

Challenges

Stand Tall

We grasp onto what we want,

It throws us to get away

We, fall.... we get up... try again... and never stray.

Again, we fall but never the same day

for we learned how to defend the old fashion way.

We grasp our opponents, in our mind or real life

And wrestle them down with verbosity and strife

With our experience getting sharper than a knife.

The master calls us as we gather around,

Giving us wisdom, never putting us down,

Showing us firmness and kindness too,

Blending thoughts and emotions the many and the few.

And again, we fight for what we believe,

with tenacity and force using balance and simplicity.

The wiser we become, yet we still take a fall,

we get up, try again, and then we stand tall.

To Give Thee

Math? Dear God, who thought of such a gift?

Square Roots, Trig, and Calculous?

I'm ready to take a fit.

If addition and subtraction weren't enough,

Some guys come up with fractions

and other confusing stuff.

My mind in abeyance, confusion and fear

Knowing only that this life

Centers on numbers and dares.

Yet, within this confusion, with numbers abound

Comes logic and life's simple pleasures...

Like roller coasters and planes that go round and round.

I may not be good at Math, you see,

But math has always been good to me.

It gave me these years to bargain and plea

How life is so filled with both sorrow and glee.

Yet numbers confusing, a hodge pod for me,

But without them there could never be

The years of love for you, and the joy I try to give thee.

Conscience

The longer we live the wiser we are.

Starting as infants, then soon driving a car.

We look to our ancestors, and parents, too,

with cometic roll models, or those considered true blue.

And as we age, and walk along the way

we ponder, we decide how will I survive with a job or trade?

I see the things that life has made,

Tantalizing, attractive, sometimes, sharp as a blade.

What do I choose? Who do I choose? When do I choose?

How do I choose? and, oh, is it correct to choose?

All these decisions I must make on my own,

the right ones come easy, but others are unknown.

I question my motives, "do I want it, or need it?"

If I get it, regardless of how it is done,

Will I regret the desire, and end up being the sad one?

Which decision is right? the choice is mine.

Just follow your conscience all the time.

Fortitude

Life presents us with challenges that include...

Some thoughts, and dreams that can change our
mood,

A change that will take us away or set an attitude.

At times confusion gets in the way,

causing us to scamper and not stay.

In those times we must settle our mind....

so, our patience doesn't fray.

Two thoughts or more come in, they loop and loop,

We constantly struggle to find the right route,

not sure what to choose, I need a parachute!

Yet in all this muck and mire and mixed up soup

difficult decisions must be made,

Which way to go? Which one to choose?

for an answer We turn to the best tool we have used

That, my friend, is intestinal fortitude.

Never say good-bye

I never thought this day would come
For years and years, we beat our own drums.
We laughed, we dined, we cried, and we whined,
But, in the end we always got entwined.

We promised each other we'd always be
The only one we each would see,
a heart emboldened is not for me.

Those deep brown eyes, and mind so wise
with arms embracing, the end is nigh.
And if our love be pure and true
Cupid's arrow pierces our hearts through and
through.

Though thoughts and wishes are set so high,
Holding each other, gazing at the bright blue sky,
We have a friendship never to die
And I just can't not love her,
I shall never say good-bye!

153

Both Have Won

A dad and his son sat one day
He asked him what he wanted to be someday
The boy looked up in astonishment
For he already had numerous accomplishments.

And in his wisdom, the dad sat still,
For the first time in his life the boy voiced his will.
"a cop," the boy said, "no, wait... a fireman, too."
But he couldn't be both. What should he do?

And so, the dad sat him down on a chair,
Speaking to him gently yet firmly with no fear,
"My son..." the dad said, "the decision is yours."
"There is nothing to fear, open many doors."

The boy grew up, and after Dad was gone.
He remembered his voice as life went on,
He opened many doors, a few slammed shut
But the one stayed open, kept him out of a rut.
Success came his way, and he, too, has a son
Imparting the same wisdom realizing both have won.

Now You Decided

Life is complex, I think we agree
Tumult in the world, and many cop a plea.
We need to think quick, and not let things be
Never acting rashly, but clearly we must see.

School work is due, and the job has issues too.
There are bills on the table, with cash to pay a few.
Many questions arise, the answers are disguised
With more demands as the day flies by.

So, take a deep breath, exhale slowly and just let go.
Look at all your options, take your time, don't rush,
Weigh each thing carefully, not with disgust,
Remembering that accuracy is indeed a must.

It's time to choose, you may look and revise.
Choose carefully and always be wise.
For good judgment is not blindsided,
Take your time, and now, you decided.

Compete

You don a uniform for all to see.

Recognition is meant to be

Standing so proudly in front of the crowd,

Hearing cheers of admiration with applauds so loud.

Standing straight, standing tall, having not a question

Not one at all, just an eye on the prize displayed on the
wall.

And soon silence looms amongst the masses

It feels like a dozen hours passes

And from a dark corner where drapes hide a door

A menacing person in uniform walks onto the floor.

Both stand before each other, intimidating to see,

Neither cracks a smile, no one shakes at the knee.

The referee reads the rules aloud

And then the contenders address the crowd.

This is the first time the two do meet,

Both look for flaws and, in danger, ways to retreat.

For now, it is time for these men to compete.

Farewell

We meet so many people, as life traverses by.

Some of those we love, whereas others we despise.

Going through life we have fantasies and dreams

Then come events that make us shout and scream.

And then there are those coming into our lives

Embrace them often and dig a few jibes.

We laugh with them and cry with them

They are our perfect gem.

Just when we think we have it all

Life goes and throws us a nasty curve ball.

We grow older, or drift away

And move forward hoping for a better day.

As we look back at life's citadel

We might view the webs Html,

On bended knee thanking God for good times,

And bidding the bad, farewell!

God and I Love You

Amongst the galaxies and stars eternal blush

Between the darkness and cosmic stuff,

The colors of a nebula's gaseous fluff

New life is introduced in this universal gush.

Tumult and swirls, bright purple, red and green

A beauty that very few have seen.

Where did it come from? Where does it go?

Into the darkness? Traversing fast or slow?

To the edge of the unknown, lies new beginnings and homes

Impossible to fathom, good God, we're not alone.

Our mind can take us to places we've never been.

With love in our heart that will never dim.

Out there, in here, our universe lies

We muse with laughter sometime with tears in our eyes.

No matter what you think, you say, or do

In this vast glorious universe God and I love you.

Challenges

"The world is your oyster," Will Shakespeare did write,

Spoken by the merry wives of Windsor

With thoughts held so tight.

A metaphor your see, not the oyster for me,

But shear hope that inside that hard shell,

A pearl so priceless will be.

The message for you, and the message for me

Is always to seek, and forever just "be."

Fight the good fight, but choose your battle well,

Lest you find yourself, a blaze in hell.

Lives filled with balances, fear not, take the plunge.

I promise you this, excitement will come,

Always seeking the pearl of wisdom

And all Challenges with a pint of rum!

Part 10

Wisdom

The Beginnings of Wisdom

When we were young, impulsiveness sprung.

In our adolescents, discovery shot forth like a gun.

Then came middle age and we learned how to have fun.

But nothing can compare to old age where years of
hardship began our road to wisdom.

So here we sit, or stand, or walk,

In silent meditation listening only to the eagle hawk.

And as we go deep, deep within

We look, we seek, we center in

If we sit so still, and listen really hard,

To that silent voice inside so dim

It will soon peal forth with an incessant hymn

Guiding and showing us

The beginnings of wisdom.

Choice

How do I decide what is best for me?

Do I listen to you, or just let things be?

If I see something desirous is it a need or a want?

And where do I go in this overwhelming hunt?

The hardest thing in life thus far

Is searching for happiness not found in a jar,

But, rather in observing, lust from afar

And wishing upon a single night star.

Do I choose red, yellow, or blue?

Am I attracted to you, or to you?

Is this job right, it feels too new?

How will I know what is true?

Stop for a moment, and look what you have done

Queries and questions looking for answers and getting none.

Just calm yourself, friend, breathe in an out

Decide if what you seek is a need or a doubt,

And then make a choice, that's what life is about.

The Seat of Wisdom

From Solomon's throne, to one who builds with stone,

No matter how powerful or skilled if left alone,

Our strength and life that we all condone

Began many generations from our family home.

We learn to think, to speak and love

In times of muddling, a philosopher we become,

As life traverses on, much reading we do,

And listening to our elders' stories,

We hold them with pride because they are true.

Then one day someone looks to you,

And asks you for words that will get them through,

You think and ponder, thinking back on days gone by.

And gently with cautious words you advise.

So, from Old Solomon's kingdom,

Look how far you have come,

Claiming your income on the Seat of Wisdom.

The Joy of Wisdom

It is said that wisdom comes with age,

Not degrees or accolades.

Traversing the winding road of joy and pain.

Mistakes we will make along the way

And learn from them as we go astray.

Then upon our return from foolish banter,

We awaken to a new life of joy and laughter.

And when troubles come our way,

Much wiser we are to keep them at bay.

Folks will look at us and ask us how,

From one day to the next we stick to our vows.

And so, we speak of our journey long past,

With the learnings and surprises we amassed.

Queries come they are the custom that lasts,

And in the quiet humble mind we hold

The joy of wisdom with words that sear the human
soul.

The Making of Wisdom

When you make wine to start with a vine,

Then trim it, and shape it, training it for next time.

Then watch the leaves slowly grow,

Bursts of green that overflow,

And soon from the shoots small buds of grapes do come,

Then when ripened to the sun you harvest and then all done.

However, with wisdom, it's a little bit more fun,

We grow with experience and maybe not the sun.

It takes more than a season but needs much fertilized care,

Then over time, not just a season wisdom appears.

The nice thing about wisdom is time,

It grows and is harvested and doesn't cost a dime.

The process is slow, but the reward is fine

That's the making of wisdom that lasts a lifetime.

The Great Wise Man

Mark Twain once wrote this, but I must warn you it
doesn't rhyme. He said:

"Never argue with stupid people, they will drag you
down to their level and then beat you with experience"
all the time.

It's easy to anger, to fuss to and frow

And just as easy to be silent and grow.

So, in the mist of tumult and peace,

Where does wisdom lie in the mired peace?

A picture we draw on the beach in the sand,

Maybe a castle, from a small coffee can.

Then once the masterpiece meets our demand,

We sit and observe what we made by hand.

In life we experiment, we design from life's demands.

'tween tumult and joy sharing wisdom's grain of sand.

Then you are noticed by a young humble fan

Who seeks only the wisdom of the great wise man.

The Great Wise Woman

In pondering, perpetual, persistent ways
With kindness and knowledge and humble accolades,
Hidden wisdom that is challenged by man
Only to find that the woman really can!

She studies, she struggles, she meets tremendous demands.
Multitasking, re-masking, taping breaks in the plan.
She's a healer, a listener, solid pilar of strength,
She'll ponder, she'll wander, and then comes the break.

Without timing nor warning, a heart goes into mourning
And upon the shoulder rests a head with tears storming
Oh, help me deal lady, I don't know what to do,
I live in life's tumult, circling like a potato in a stew.

With kind eyes and a gentle hand,
She rises to meet this sorrowful demand.
And drawing deep from within
The Great Wise Woman teaches courage to the man.

The Seeker of Wisdom

Plato, Aristotle, and Socrates we know,

Emmanuel Kant, John Stewart Mill,

True philosophers we teach about and show.

All have looked deeply into themselves and the world

Centering carefully in,

Pondering, concerning, blending thoughts in the cosmic winds.

We learn to think critically, answer questions so deep

Surrendering only to those secrets asleep.

We ask many questions, few answers are heard,

But in our deep bursting hearts there is no word.

In subtle silence we ponder well

Shall we be The Seeker of Wisdom? Only time will tell.

Sophia

The Greeks have a word, Wisdom is her name.

She shines and she glimmers

She never hides in shame.

She speaks from experience

All night and all day

And her words so brilliant, will never go away.

Her name is Sophia,

In seeking her wisdom, we will always find our way.

Divine Wisdom

We live in a world of scientific wonder.

TV shows us an evolving world out of great thunder.

Gasses are formed, stars are born

Rocks are hurled and planets form with storms.

From the deepest avenues of space out there

Flies' minerals, gems, and water.

As in the tumult of speed, and spin, and crash and calm,

We hear arguments saying that is where we are from.

The earth, we're told, was filled with deadly gases, and lots
of crater holes, tossed about in logical masses.

Soon water and amoebas grew.

And then one day, and no one knows how or where,

Came an upright man with lots of hair.

From nothing came something, or was something always
there?

No matter the answer, all of us found our way here.

We still are evolving, being created and shaped,

And one day... long, long away, shall come,

We shall find our roots

In the heart of Divine Wisdom.

Wisdom

I wonder, I ponder, I philosophize too.

I analyze carefully, working difficulties through.

It starts with a query, and ends with a rhyme,

Not understanding what's happening all the time.

Soon, if I'm lucky, an answer will come,

Slowly, slithering, from the somnambulance's memory throng.

And, then in a quiet, quintessential quip

Comes an answer to that queries secret grip.

Like racing greyhounds about the dusty track,

Our heart and thoughts race boldly experiencing life's gentle dip.

The questions come and the truth is near,

Relentlessly impeding our minds with an alogism of fear.

We realize in silence, we may even shed a tear

With no rhyme nor rhythm

We discover Wisdom was always there.

Part 11

Haiku

Ran

Orchid

Beautiful, Vibrant, alive, colorful, and royal

Orchid

蝶

Butterfly

Strongly delicate, gliding with the wind

Butterfly

Yanagi no ki

柳の木

Willow Tree

Old, Bent, Yet proud

Willow Tree,

Maiagaru washi

舞い上がる鷲

Soaring Eagle,
Vigilant Protector and defender
Soaring Eagle

Geisha

芸者

Geisha

Compassion, Patience and Joy

Geisha

Doragon

ドラゴン

Dragon

Fierce, Fiery, Fury

Dragon

Tora

虎

Tiger

Quiet, Calculating, Vigilant

Tiger

Uma

馬

Horse

Powerful, Speedy Carrier

Horse

Tori ni esa o yaru

鳥に餌をやる

Feeding Bird
Perched, Receiving Life
Feeding Bird

Bushi

武士

Samurai

Meditative, Unsuspecting,

Deadly Guardian

Samurai

Kirihanasenai

切り離せない

Inseparable

Two perched in love

Inseparable

Inochi no goburetto

命のゴブレット

Goblet of Life

Filled with dreams, hopes, journeys, and good wine

Goblet of Life

Gō rudofinchi

ゴールドフィンチ

Goldfinch
Perched upon a grapevine,
Colorful and gentle
Golden gem of the Earth
Goldfinch

Taida

怠惰

Sloth

Slow, unassuming.

Avoidant and lazy

Smiles while dreaming peacefully

Sloth

Botan

牡丹

Peony

Red and Beautiful

Observe and admire

In beautiful harmony with nature

Peony

Ō *mu*

オウム

Parrot
Colorful, Delightful to the eye
At peace in love,
Guardian to his wife
Parrot

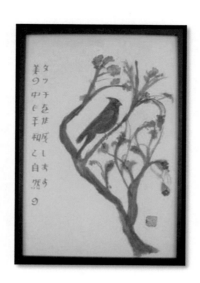

Sukikyō

枢機卿

Cardinal
Both red bird and holy man
Bright colors that command respect
Cardinal

Hezā

ヘザー

Heather

Flower dancing on a mountain

Bright colors please the eye

Heather

Heaven

(Tengoku)

Heaven

Joy, Peace, and Love

God's Home

Heaven

Ocean

(Taiyo)

大洋

Ocean

Holds hidden life

Ocean

Banyon Tree

(Gajumarunoki)

ガジュマルの木

Banyon Tree

Roots of life to see

Haven for the creatures

Banyon Tree

Island

(Shimauchi)

Island

Trees, Sand, and Water

Island

<u>Altar</u>

<u>(Saidan)</u>

祭壇

Altar

Table, majestic and old

Altar

Two birds

(Ni wanotori)

二羽の鳥

Two birds

Perched, observant, singing

Two birds

Companions

(Tomodachi)

仲間

Companions

Loving, Trusting, Caring

Companions

Throne

(Oi)

王座

Throne

Seat of service, cloth and wood

Throne

<u>Bull</u>

(Buru)

ブル

Bull

Unsuspecting, Guardian, Protector

Bull

Illuminate

(Terasu)

照らす

Illuminate

Guiding sparkles of light

Illuminate

About the Author

Born in Philadelphia, Pennsylvania, in 1958, Tony Scuderi earned several Doctoral Degrees. He has a Doctor of Divinity in Theology, a Doctor of Ministry in Marriage and Family, and a Doctor of Psychology, and a Doctor of Interjurisdictional Canon Law. At the time of this publication, he teaches Canon Law and is Dean of the School of Canon Law, through the Meister Eckhart Divinity School. He practices as an Interjurisdictional Canon lawyer when needed and is the Justice on the Interjurisdictional Canon Law Court. He has written 15 textbooks in Canon Law and has written the Text and Commentary of the Code of Canon Law for the Ecumenical Catholic Church of Chrit (RCCC), and a Pontifical for Bishops in the ECCC, where he is the Metropolitan Archbishop of California, Apostolic Nuncio for the United States (Diplomatic Ambassador for the Church), Dean of Students and Formation, and the Minister Provincial for the New Order of St. Francis. Dr. Tony is also a Certified Addictions and Relationship Life Coach and Certified Hypnotherapist through the American Institute of Hypnotherapy and Psychotherapy in New York.

He has over 30 years of experience in the Behavioral Science and addiction fields. He is certified by the California Consortium of Addictions Programs and Professionals (CCAPP) as a Licensed Advanced Alcohol and Drug Counselor-Supervisor, Certified Criminal Justice Professional, and Certified Co-occurring disordered professional. Throughout his career as a Mental Health and Substance Abuse professional, Dr. Tony has held numerous clinical positions ranging from line therapist to CEO and Private Practitioner. He has taught academically at such colleges/universities as Immaculata University, Pennsylvania; Newman College, Pennsylvania, University of California-Berkeley Extension; University of San Francisco; and presently for InterCoast College. He has and does teach courses in the General and Clinical Psychology Field for both undergraduate and graduate students, the entire addictions studies curriculum for ICC, with specialties in Group and Individual Counseling techniques, Anatomy, Physiology, Neurology, and Pharmacology, along with teaching. By appointment, he is starting a new private practice in addiction counseling and life coaching. For fun, he holds a 10th Degree Black Belt in Judo from the All Japan Jujitsu International Federation (AJJIF), a 10th Degree Black Belt in Jujitsu, and a 7th Degree Black Belt in Aikijitsu (AJJIF), and he enjoys playing the Tenor Banjo, Guitar, Piano, Violin, and Mandolin. In addition to these, Dr. Tony does Japanese Watercolors, makes wine, and is a HAM Radio Operator (General Class KM6GMS).